Cake Decorating for Beginners
Tips and Ideas for Cakes Made Easy

Table of Contents

Chapter 1

Introduction

Chapter 2

Culinary School - Baking and Pastry Degree

Chapter 3

Wilton School of Cake Decorating

Chapter 4

Universal Class Online Cake Decorating

Chapter 5

A-J Winbeckler Enterprises Cake Decorating

Chapter 6

Amy Malone School of Cake Decorating

Chapter 7

"Do It With Icing!"

Chapter 8

Pattycakes School of Cake Decorating

Chapter 9

The Cake Carousel School of Cake Decorating

Chapter 10

Cake Art Cake Decorating and
Candy Making Classes

Chapter 11

Golda's Kitchen

Chapter 12

Open Directory

Chapter 13

Fabulous Foods and Cakes N Things

Chapter 1

Introduction

For some cake decorating is a hobby, and for others, it is a career. The amateurs are those who find it fun and gratifying to bake the cakes and then decorate them for their family and friend, save money by doing it themselves. With expert training along with good decorating tips and ideas, any one can master this art. With this art form you will be able to stretch your imagination. If you continue building your skills, you will experience the joy of making others happy with your expertise.

The art of decorating cakes takes place when a man or woman has turned the kitchen into an art studio. When a cake is decorated in an artistic design it is pleasing to both the creator and the recipient. Creating a cake does not have to be a stressful experience, you just need to get creative.

Don't be afraid to try new ideas and techniques. For the amateur, it is the simple cake decorating tips, which are the best ways to help you get started. Decorating can be as simple as using a stencil and dusting confectioner's sugar or cocoa powder on the top of a cake.

Cakes can be iced with butter cream, royal fondant, or cooked icing. Adding to the icing cakes can be topped with flowers, spun sugar, or candy. Cakes can be created to look like a hot dog, pizza, or just about anything you have the imagination to create.

If you want to be an amateur cake decorator, you will need to learn the basics and pick up as many of the tips you can. There are many tips and ideas widely available. You may decide to continue making and decorating cakes as a pastime or you may decide to look into making a career out of decorating and baking cakes.

The Wilton schools have several students who have a professional goal in mind. Wilton schools have classes designed for anyone who loves cake decorating. Wilton classes are taught at several local retailers through out the United States and Canada. Here are some of the Wilton school tips and hints on icing a cake.

Wilton schools prefer to use Duncan Hines cake mixes because the batter volume is the same every time you make it.

Adding a teaspoon or two of Wilton Meringue Powder to the mix will make the cake rise higher.

When preparing your pans, use a 2-inch wide paintbrush to paint on the shortening. If an area is still shiny, apply more shortening and dust with flour.

Only fill your cake pans half full.

Let your cake cool completely rest in an airtight container for a day or even overnight before you ice it.

Cut the mounded portion of the cake off with a leveler or a serrated knife to make the cake level and fit together easier.

Turn the cake over and brush the cake with a wide paintbrush to remove the crumbs.

Use a lot of icing to ice the top of the cake. Never let your spatula touch the cake. You will have crumbs in your icing if you do.

If you are having a difficult time in icing the sides of the cake, Wilton has a tip, number 789, which is made just for icing the sides of the cake.

Let the cake rest for 15 minutes after you have iced it. Then smooth out the cake by using parchment paper. To do this, place the parchment paper on the cake and gently smooth out the icing.

If you have a cake mix, which only makes one layer. Then turn it into a torte. Slice the cake horizontally. By adding a ring of icing from a decorating bag through a tip, you will be able to create a dam on the outside of the bottom half of the cake. For a filling use the pudding from a child's pudding cup, and spread it inside the ring. Top with the other half of the cake and ice as directed.

You will need to choose a source of instruction. The culinary schools are colleges and will give you a degree making you more marketable if you choose to look for employment in this line of work. However, if you just want to be an expert there are many types of schools and classes you can take to achieve this. Some of the courses can be taken on location online or you can find web sites, which will give you instruction by video or walking you through it, step-by-step.

A professional cake baker is a culinary expert who specializes in creating cakes. Most of these cakes are made for special events and weddings. There are a number of cake bakers who have their own bakeries. Cake bakers do some cake baking, whereas some pastry professional only specialize in cake decorating.

Chapter 2

Culinary School – Baking and Pastry Degree

A professional cake decorator is one who is trained in the art of creating designs on pastries and cakes. These designs can range from the simple to the elaborate. To be a cake decorator you must have an understanding of fillings and frostings in order to turn them into the beautiful works of art found on cakes. Cake decorators must also learn the temperatures certain baking materials can withstand. Some cake decorators choose to specialize in wedding cakes because there is such a huge demand for them.

There are educational requirements to become a professional cake decorator. Formal training and education is suggested if an individual is interested in becoming a cake. decorator. Many students can attend a pastry program, which is accredited by the American Culinary Federation.

There are several culinary schools for you to choose from when pursuing cake decorating as a career. Wilton school is one of the many vocational schools, which train professional and amateur cake decorators. There is also the Art Institute, Le Cordon Bleu Schools, the Florida Culinary Institute, Kendall College, Oregon Culinary Institute, Lincoln College of Technology, Arizona Culinary Institute, Capital Culinary Institute, and the Johnson & Wales University just to mention a few.

Training and education is encouraged when a person shows an interest in becoming a cake decorator or a cake baker. Most employers prefer to hire those with a certificate received from an accredited school as well as those with relevant work experience.

The occupational outlook for cake bakers and cake decorators, according to the U.S. Bureau of Labor Statistics, the economists are predicting the demand for baking careers to increase as quickly as the average. These same experts are saying most of the available positions for a cake baker or cake decorator will be in store, specialty shops and traditional bakeries. Earning in the year 2004 was $21,330, which was the middle salary reported by the U.S. Bureau of Labor Statistics.

Once you are in a culinary program you will learn how to blend color and how to create shapes. You will also learn the art of molding sugar and the uses for it. You will learn the physics used in building towers and you will acquire the ability to sketch out your projects. If it is your dream of owning your own company one day, your chosen program will include entrepreneurship and you will learn the financial facet of the business.

Your course work will depend on the college you choose since each one is different. Some of the most common courses you will probably take are:

French Math

Business Management

Inventory Control and Purchasing Tortes and Cakes

Concepts & Theories of Culinary Techniques

Purchasing

Sanitation & Safety

Cost Control

Cakes for Display

Chocolate, Confections & Centerpieces

After receiving a culinary degree in Cake Decorating you may choose to open your own bakery or cake-decorating store. You may want to take advantage of the apprenticeships available to culinary graduates who want to start their own bakeries or catering companies.

Because cake decorating is a hands-on industry, the more you practice the better your skill will become. It is a good idea for graduates to search out mentors who can work with them to build stronger culinary skills and techniques. Standard classroom settings cannot provide this type of extensive training.

The type of position you have and the region you are employed in will make a difference in your salary. A cake decorator's employment opportunities can include a pastry artisan, cake designer, bakery owner, and catering.

Baking and Pastry Arts II adds to your marketability if you have already taken Baking and Pastry Arts I. Also the additional training will give you an edge while searching for a position in an upscale establishment, which would pay very well.

If you are the type of person who likes getting up early in the morning and gets pleasure from working with their hands, a degree program in Baking and Pastry Arts can be a satisfying career. Those who have earned a certificate or degree in the Baking and Pastry

Arts can find employment as cooks, pastry chefs or bakers.

There are only some people who like baking because it is hot, backbreaking work. Plus most bakers have to get up early. But for some people baking is an opportunity to use food as a medium for their art. If you are one of those people who enjoy cooking and baking, and don't mind rising early, you will probably enjoy the pastry arts as a profession. Should you decide to major in baking and pastry arts you will spend about 15 to 40 hours per week in the kitchen included with your other coursework. You will start you day as early as 6 in the morning and learn skills such as basic bread and pastry baking, chocolatiering, meringue creation, use of icing, Continental baking, ingredient selection, menu creation, and more.

Cooks are an extensive group of workers. They generally cook and prepare food in restaurants, catering establishments, cafes, hotels and more. They must have the ability to multitask and work quickly in order to direct the tasks others. The also must have an acute sense of smell and taste along with an extensive knowledge of ingredients and of the dishes they are in charge of preparing. You will find cooks working in diner's or at 5-star establishments, but at "Billy Bob's Roadside Diner" it is not likely for you to find a graduate from Baking and Pastry Arts programs. However you will find those who have combine baking and pastry skills with all-around cooking and culinary skills in upscale establishments.

Pastry chefs are a sweet tooth's best friend. They are the people who create such items as the bear claws, fine doughnuts, specialty breads, muffins and much more. They can work on commission making desserts for special occasions, or they could own a business and produce the same type of stock every day. For the pastries businesses who deliver goods to coffee shops and stores must be ready to deliver as early as 6 or 7 in the morning. It is predicted the employment growth for bakers of all kinds will continue to grow. The middle range of salaries is from $30,000 to $40,000 for inexperienced workers and range from $44,000 to $67,000 for executive pastry chefs.

It is a common misconception among most of us, which says, bakers only bake bread, right? Stop and think about who made the tortilla wrapped around your burrito, or who made the cake your mom bought at the store? Bakers. They are responsible for the creation of many of the things we take for granted. They make pie, croissants and other items with the use of their knowledge of equipment, baking ingredients, health codes, and other standards.

Baking and Pastry Arts Degree

The Baking and Pastry Arts program will train you to become a skilled dessert chef. Through this program you will be introduced to the world of desserts and the numerous ways to create these masterpieces. Also with this training, you will learn to combine textbook techniques with creativity, and you will have the hands-on experience with kitchen tools used in a professional setting. Some of the other area covered will be the terminology used in the industry along with health and safety issues related to this line of work.

You will develop skills during the course of Baking and Pastry classes in Baking Methodology, Food Preparation, Basic Service, Plating Techniques, Creativity, and Analytical Thinking.

There are several reasons for taking the baking and pastry arts program is you will have a variety of settings to work in such as coffee shops to upscale hotels. Owning your own business is another option. There are numerous job opportunities in the baking and pastry arts, however you might want to keep in mind you will have considerable competition if you want to work for an upscale business. Your salary as a bakery and pastry chef depends on the location, level of experience, and responsibility. The average yearly salary for a bakery and pastry artist averages to be about $25 per hour.

If you have taken Baking and Pastry Arts I then you will want to take Baking and Pastry Arts II. You will use and improve your skills learned in Baking and Pastry Arts I and will make even more advanced specialty desserts and pastries. The courses you can expect to take when you take the Bakery and Pastry Arts II are:

Restaurant desserts

Advanced pastries

Menu planning

Plate Presentation

Pricing

Recipe research and evaluation

Management

Classical desserts

The courses offered depend on each individual institution. Most courses will include laboratory classes where students can obtain hand-on experience in the creation of baked goods and pastry.

The skills you will learn when taking this course are advanced pastry technique, advanced dessert creation, the correct use of equipment and utensils, safety and sanitation techniques, working in a team atmosphere, organizational skills, presentation skills, timing skills, and a la carte skills.

Chapter 3

Wilton School of Cake Decorating

The Wilton School of Cake Decorating and Confectionary Art

You don't have to have a degree in baking and pastry arts to become an expert cake decorator. You just want to become an expert.

There are several accredited schools you can receive training from to become an expert at cake decorating. Wilton school is just one of the most well known. There are even classes for cake decorating you can take online.

The Wilson School of Cake Decorating and Confectionary Art is a private vocational school. When it comes to cake decorating, Wilson school has been the leader in cake decorating education throughout the world for generations. In 1929 Dewey McKinley Wilton first began teaching his now famous Wilton Method. The mission of the Wilton school is to provide quality in cake decorating education. The school started on age-old cake decorating traditions, but is constantly enhanced by increasing and refining creativity. Mr. Wilton's philosophy is "learning is best achieved through class participation." This educational approach is still alive in today's expanded Wilton School faculty along with the curriculum and advanced techniques Here the Wilton Method Classes are described.

Course I – Cake Decorating

During a Wilton Method Class many people will have the opportunity to experience the excitement of decorating their first cake. Your instructor will show you step by step, ways to decorate your cakes and desserts. As you learn new decorating techniques you will have other students encouraging you as you will be encouraging them. Learning new decorating techniques will also give a sense of pride in your accomplishments, and you will be able to share your accomplishments with your friends and family.

Course II – Flowers and More

This course will build on the skills you learned in course I. Your instructor will introduce you to many techniques, which will make your cakes memorable. Master the technique of making elegant bouquets, which will feature rosettes, reverse shells, and rope designs. These techniques will give your cakes an astonishing dimension with the addition of bold colorful decorations. Learn to create new flowers like rosebuds, daisies, daffodils, mums, and more. By using the interwoven basket weave technique, you can use these flowers to make a grand flower basket cake.

Course III – Fondant and Tiered Cakes

With this course you will learn a new level of decorating with flowers and techniques. You begin with the detailed designs such as the embroidery, the lace, etc. You will notice the beauty of decorating with rolled fondant to cover the cake with a smooth surface. You will have fun shaping figures and beautiful flowers to adorn your cake. Add new flowers to your collection and include some holiday blooms like the poinsettia and the Easter lily. You will complete your course by constructing and decorating a towering tiered cake with lovely borders, flowers, and string work.

During this time you can take a project class. In this class you will have only one project to decorate. Some of your choices will be pre-baked Gingerbread Houses, Fondant Cakes, Star Character Cakes, Blossoms, Mini Cakes, Candy and more.

At the Wilton school there are one-day and three-day workshops as well as additional classes you can take to perfect your art. The one-day workshops are designs not only for the serious decorators, but the new decorators also. These classes will include the Art of Sweet Tables, Baking Workshop, Basics of Cake Icing and Decorating, and Brittles and More, just to name a few.

The three-day workshops will give you, the student, the opportunity to focus on specific decorating and baking controls. Some of these classes will include Advanced Fondant Art, Cake Decorating Camp for Kids, and Cake Sculpting, just to name a few.

Some of the Advanced Decorating Courses include Advanced Sugar Artistry, Building and Decorating Real Tiered Cakes, Chocolate Inspiration 1 & 2, and Gum Paste just to name a few.

Here are some of the classes offered at the Wilton school. The Master Course, Introduction to Rolled Fondant, Introduction to Sugar Artistry, and Introduction to Gum Paste.

The Master Course is a professional course for teachers, bakers, caterers, chefs, and beginners. This course is intended to prepare students for a career in cake decorating. This course will teach basic techniques to design and decorate party cakes and a decorated 3-tiered display wedding cake. The students will do all the actual decorating with supervision. The students will learn to make 15 flowers and 20 different borders.

The students in this course will also have the opportunity to sign up for the additional classes listed above. These additional classes are offered during the Master Course, which lasts about 2 weeks. This course is also offered to those who work. The Master Course is available on the weekend. All supplies for these classes are furnished.

The Master Course schedule

Day 1:

Orientation and the introduction to cake decorating

Demonstrations for making royal and boiled icings

Torte, and fill and ice 8" cake for wedding cake assembly demonstration

Star borders, fill-in and dots

Curving lines, vines, stems and leaves

Zigzags, rosettes, emotion and shell borders

Day 2:

Practice techniques from day before

Shell and reverse shell border

Rope and String work designs

Zigzag and ruffle garlands

Tiered wedding cake assembly

Basket weave design

Crown, chandelier and reverse chandelier borders

Day 3

Practice techniques learned from day before

Fence border and lattice garland

Drop flowers, sweet peas and rosebuds

Bows, rose bases and roses

Day 4

Practice techniques learned from day before

Wild roses, daisies, and daffodils

Easter lilies and petunias

Day 5

Practice techniques learned from day before

Prepare Styrofoam dummies

Poinsettias, pansies and carnations

Rose review

Lilies of the valley

Day 6

Flower making for wedding cakes

Mums and bachelor buttons

Writing and printing

Flower spray on cake circle

Demo for wiring and chalk dusting flowers

Day 7

More flower making for wedding cakes

Figure piping

Booties, pins, rattles and diapers

Storks, swans and hearts

Clowns

Day 8

More flower making for wedding cakes

Color flow

Piping gel

12" sampler birthday cake

Day 9

Assemble and decorate an individual 3-tiered wedding cake

Day 10

Tour Wilton Headquarters Specialty demonstrations

Graduation

Packing of cakes

Wilton schools is just one of the ways for someone to learn cake decorating. For those of you unable or lack the time to attend the formal classroom training by Wilton. Wilton classes are taught at Michael's and other cake-decorating retailers. If you are looking to improve your skills as a cake decorator, this is just one of the other options you have. With Wilton school you can learn as much as you want. If you are looking to become an expert in the cake-decorating field or if you are just a beginner, Wilton has something for you.

Chapter 4

Universal Class Online Cake Decorating

Universal Class Online Cake Decorating provides additional training, which can also be received online. With this course you will receive an online copy and a hardcopy of Certificate of Course Completion, which will display your coursework. The coursework for this program is:

Lesson 1 – Getting started includes making sure you have all the right equipment and tools to decorate cakes.

Lesson 2 – Cake Baking Basics – You will learn the proper way to bake a cake for you to decorate.

Lesson 3 – Decorating your cake using Butter Cream icing

Lesson 4 – Decorating your cake using Royal icing

Lesson 5 – Decorating your cake with sugar flowers, and other gum paste creations.

Lesson 6 – Decorating children's cakes

Lesson 7 – Decorating holiday and celebration cakes

Lesson 8 – Learning the recipes for yellow cake, chocolate cake, the classic white layer cake, butter cream icing, royal icing, marzipan, rolled fondant, and gum paste.

The course is only provided for your personal enhancement. This course is not meant to teach you to be a professional cake decorator.

For more information see universalclass.com

Chapter 5

A-J Winbeckler Enterprises Cake Decorating

A-J Winbeckler Enterprises Cake Decorating has a professional class and a student class. There are several different types of training you can choose from. These classes will give you a great beginning or add to your existing knowledge.

The 4-Day Courses

Professional Decorating Course

This course will cover color mixing, border, flowers, and the basic use of an airbrush, cupcake figure piping, wedding cake theory, and 3-D cake cartooning. Also included are the rules of art, writing, realistic piping of faces and figures, and a lot more. The locations of the class will affect the cost, class scheduling, etc.

4-Day Cake Sculpture Course

This course will teach you how to make full-relief, stand-up cake sculpture plus wire-frame sculptures, cone-figure sculptures, and sculptured piping. During this course each student will complete 3 stand-up cake sculptures plus many small sculptures.

4-Day Airbrush Course

In this course you will learn the correct way to operate an airbrush. You will also learn how to make and use stencils, create special effects, and do lifelike portraits.

2-Day Courses

2-Day Sculpture Course

This course includes sculptured figure piping for the making of realistic faces and figures. You will also make a stand-up cake sculpture from Styrofoam.

2-Day Flowers, Wedding Cake, and Borders Course

This course will teach you several flowers including two types of mums, poinsettia, daffodil, and rose. All flowers are made with butter cream icing on a skewer or directly on a cake. Also included are practical wedding cake design and setup and practical borders.

2-Day Figure Piping Course

This course includes cute figures, which are perfect for cupcakes and larger cakes. Figures include bubblehead figures, and 3-D cartooning. 3-D cartooning figures will cover an entire cake.

2-Day Floral Arrangement, Writing, And Ice Cream Cone Figure Course

In this course you will learn foliage for arrangements and you will create an orchid arrangement. Also you will learn to make a holiday arrangement with pinecones, evergreen boughs, and candles. You will also improve on your writing skills and learn the Old English form of writing along with calligraphy, bubble-style writing, oriental-style writing, and more. You will create in class a cute figure piped onto an ice cream cone.

2-Day Airbrush Course

In this course you will learn the proper use and care of an airbrush. You will learn how to do shading, how to fog cake edges, and how to create attractive borders. You will also learn to make and use stencils and the rules of airbrush portraiture.

For those who work and are unable to attend classes during the day there are classes available in the evening. These are the classes offered in the evening.

Cocoa Painting Class

Learn to create attractive cocoa paintings, in both the brown tones and in colors. Various different backgrounds will be covered.

Wafer Paper Uses Class

You will learn to transfer patterns of wafer paper butterflies, wafer paper sugar painting and techniques for making rice paper flowers and lifelike fall leaves.

Rolled Butter Cream Icing Class

You will learn to cover a cake with rolled butter cream icing. You will also learn how to pipe with it, mold with it, crimping with it, embossing with it, and much more.

Fancy Borders Class

You will learn to create a variety of elegant borders using basic decorating tips. The borders can be used on sheet cakes and wedding cakes.

Chapter 6

Amy Malone School of Cake Decorating

The Amy Malone School of Cake Decorating has classes for Beginners and up. These classes are held in LaMesa, California. You will find classes to fit your every need if your interest is in becoming an expert cake decorator.

Cake Decorating for Beginners

In this course you will learn professional baking hints, how to evenly bake and level cakes. You will also learn the method of smoothly frosting cake, four borders used in decorating cakes, precise latticework, and roses. You will also cover drop flowers, leaves, color flow, sugar molded baby booties, baskets, black cats and royal icing daisies. Piping a floral spray, pattern transfer, corneilli lace work, use of a template, figure piping of clowns, and even how to price cakes are just some of the skills you will learn during this six week course. Professional food presentation is emphasized in order for students to learn to adapt their skills to cream cheese, butter, chocolate whipped cream and mashed potatoes.

Easy Fun with Chocolate

This is a course teaching you how to dip Oreo and other store-bought cookies in white and dark chocolate. You will learn to decorate them to look like tuxedos and bridal dresses with fondant pearls. You will mold chocolate flowers, wedding cakes, pumpkins, skulls, Christmas trees, holly leaves, booties, rattles hearts, rabbits, and bells to be used in decorating the cookies. You will also learn to double-dip strawberries and assist in completing a stylish strawberry tree centerpiece.

Hors d' oeuvres

In this course you will make cheese-filled phyllo triangles, Crab Remick dip, BLT-stuffed cherry tomatoes, and a Christmas tree shaped ham and cheese spread. You will also learn to fill deviled eggs with a pastry bag. Advanced preparation and attractive presentation is emphasized.

Fun Fall Cupcakes & More

In this course you will learn to decorate cupcakes with the use of figure piping witches, ghosts, spiders, pumpkins, Santa Claus faces, wreaths, and Christmas trees. You will also learn the methods to neatly frost a cupcake in 5 seconds. You will learn to adapt your skills to decorate cookies; sugar cubes, mints, and larger cakes will be covered. Also learn to use an airbrush, stencil, figure piping and rice paper techniques to decorate a haunted house sheet cake.

Garnishes

In this course you will make apple birds, orange baskets, carrot spirals, cucumber chains, egg chickens, radish mushrooms, cucumber twigs, fluted mushrooms, and more. The making of butter roses will be demonstrated.

Cream Puffs, Éclairs & Napoleons

An Instructor will demonstrate how to make Napoleons and mix, form, bake and fill cream puffs with crème patisserie, and ice cream. You as the student will fill pastries, and dip them in chocolate. Savory fillings such as chicken salad with nuts, mushroom, and crab will be featured, and the recipes for both sweet and savory fillings and chocolate glazes are included.

Gingerbread House Workshop

This is a two-part course where you will learn to mix, bake, cut, and assemble and decorate a charming gingerbread house using royal icing and candies. The candies used will be gumdrops, Red Hots, Lifesavers, nuts, mints, Starbursts, Necco Wafers, jelly beans, spearmint leaves, caramels, marshmallow toys, candy canes, Tootsie Rolls, edible glitter and more. The instructor will demonstrate every step and complete a multicolored decorated small house with outside snowy scenery in the first session. You will bake pieces at home to assemble and decorate in the second session. The methods for making icing icicles and ice cream cone Christmas trees will be covered.

Peek-a-boo 3-D Cookie Holiday Greeting Cards

This workshop will teach you how to make a unique 3D greeting card. You will learn how to bake Christmas tree-shaped sugar cookies and to assemble them into freestanding folded two-piece cards, and then to decorate them by using royal icing and fondant. You will hand-mold a fondant Santa to peek through the windowed front. You will be using a luster dust to create shiny gold stars and ribbons on cookie packages.

Cookies, Cookies, Cookies

In this course, you will learn how to make gingersnaps coated with crystal sugar, rich fudge foggies, and flower shaped raspberry-filled Lizner cookies. You will also learn to make lemon-flavored pizelles, meringue clusters with chocolate chips, and peppermint candy. Holiday gift ideas and presentation is emphasized. Shade and enhance picccs petal dusts will be used during demonstration.

Cookie Bouquets

In this course you will mix, roll perfect thickness, cut, skewer, bake, decorate, assemble and arrange cookies into gifts or centerpieces for holidays and celebrations, such as Valentine's Day, birthdays, bridal and baby showers, Easter, Super Bowl and other special sporting events. Advanced and beginner decorating techniques will be used.

Marzipan Fruits and Animals

You will make marzipan mice, puppy dogs, ducks, grapes, pumpkins, oranges, lemons, bananas, pears, strawberries, carrots, apples, and baked potatoes.

Vegetable Flower Centerpieces

This course will include detailed instructions in the creation of flowers made from vegetables into centerpieces. You will learn the cutting, assembling, and arranging of the vegetable orchids, calla lilies, apple blossoms, daisies, daffodils, wild roses, mums, pansies, dahlias, anthuriums, fantasy flowers, and much more. You will be using radishes, red cabbage, turnips, scallions, carrots, baby corn, green peppers, broccoli, olives, and squash. You and the other students will create more than a dozen flowers to take home. You will also learn to adapt the bouquets to birthdays, bridal showers, flowers and the use of edible markers. You will learn to use rolled fondant as a base.

Cupcakes: Baking Basics and Beyond

You will learn how to bake, fill and frost identical looking cupcakes. Learn the method to evenly distribute batter. Learn how to hollow out cupcakes and fill with chocolate mousse, whipped butter pecan filling, cinnamon sugar cream cheese filling and lemon curd. You will learn to frost your cupcakes with a candy coating and flavored glazes.

Wedding Cake Workshop

This is a two-part class where you will learn to bake, frost, dowel, assemble, decorate and transport a three-tier wedding cake. You will be given step-by-step detailed instructions and they will all be demonstrated on the first night. You will bake your cake at home to be assembled and decorated in class on the second night.

Cookie Decorating for Spring

You will learn to use royal icing to decorate hearts, Easter eggs and wedding cake shaped sugar cookies. You will learn the method of outlining, flooding, stenciling, single and double feathering, 3-D lattice cages, drop instruction on the art of cake decorating. These classes will include many of the same things covered by the other schools and probably some that were not covered.

Chapter 7

"Do It With Icing!"

"Do It With Icing!" is another cake decorating school where holidays, and other occasions will be emphasized.

Christmas Candy 2

Workshop with Linda Bills

If you think you have learned all you can about chocolate, come and see what you might have missed. This class will show you special chocolate treats and new techniques such as "painting" chocolate into molds to achieve professional multi-colored results. You will learn to make easy turtles, caramel truffles, chocolate covered cherries, piped chocolate designs to go on top of your desserts, the use of chocolate transfer sheets, along with chocolate creations as time permits. You will learn packaging, coloring, and use of sparkling dusting powders.

Christmas Cookie Blowout
Workshop with Susan Carberry

Christmas is the time for cookies. Learn how to create fabulous holiday sugar cookies to give as Christmas gifts or to decorate your holiday table. These cookies will even look good decorating your Christmas tree. Fondant and Royal Icing will be used to create these delectable, festive delights.

Christmas Fondant Characters
Workshop with Susan Carberry

In this course you will make fun holiday characters, which will be used on upcoming cakes or gingerbread houses. You will make a small Christmas Scene, which will include a fondant Reindeer, Snowman & Santa. Fondant and royal icing will be used to create the tinting in theses holiday creations.

Intermediate Cake Decorating with Linda Bills

This course is for those you have had a basic class or have taught themselves the basics. The instructor, Linda, will review roses to start and progress to daisies, pansies, daffodils, wild roses, violet and other flowers. Figure piping will be done as well as some cakes with cut out shapes or 3-D designs.

Chapter 8

Pattycakes School of Cake Decorating

Pattycakes is another school offering classes in baking and cake decorating. The classes are by types of instruction you would want to learn.

The Cake Decorating Course is 12 Classes of 3 hours each. It covers cake decorations, flowers, tiered cakes, and color flow.

The Advanced Fondant Course is 4 Classes of 3 hours each. It covers sugar decorations, laces, drapes, flowers, and extension work.

The Gum Paste Flowers Course is 4 Classes of 3 hours each. It covers the making of flowers, such as Hibiscus, Tulip, Iris, Orchid, Roses, Lily, Calla Lily, and many more.

Airbrush Technique Course is 3 Classes. It covers all techniques and uses of an airbrush.

Dominican Decorations is 5 Classes. Boiled icing decorations such as shirt, basket, crib, gifts and wedding.

Baking Classes

Cookies – 4-hour class. It covers chocolate chip, oatmeal raisin, ginger cookies, vanilla butter cookies, and Madeline.

Candy-Chocolate cake – 4 ½ hours. It covers lollipops, candy chocolates, ganache, and old-fashioned chocolate cake.

Pound cake – jellyroll – 4 hours. It covers vanilla pound cake, jellyroll, Italian Meringue, ganache, simple syrup, and Chantilly.

Fruit cake (Black cake) – 4 ½ hours. It covers royal icing, black cake covered with marzipan and fondant, basic fondant for beginners.

Dominican cake - 4 hours. Cake from scratch, filling, frosting, syrup, basic decorating for beginners.

Filling & Frosting – 4 hours. It covers chocolate mousse, Italian meringue, French butter cream, American butter cream, jams, cream cheese filling, and royal icing.

Tres Leches & Cheese cake – 4 ½ hours. It covers Tres leches cake, cheesecake, Chantilly, Italian meringue, and graham cracker crust.

Cupcakes & Brownies – 4 hours. It covers vanilla cupcakes, chocolate cupcakes, ganache, vanilla frosting, and brownies.

Red Velvet Cake – 4 hours. It covers cake from scratch, cream cheese frosting, and basic decorating for beginners.

Carrot cake & Pineapple Upside Down cake – 4 hours. It covers cake from scratch, cream cheese frosting, and Chantilly.

Chapter 9

The Cake Carousel School of Cake Decorating

The Cake Carousel is another school offering instructions on cake decorating and other instructions related to this industry. This school is located in North Texas. The curriculum also has classes for beginners, intermediate and advanced students.

Cake Decorating Classes

Basic Cake Decorating is a 5-session course, which focuses on the demonstration of basic tools to begin cake decorating; including hints for making icing and baking cakes. You will also learn how to level, tort, fill and frost the cake. You will learn top, side and bottom borders. Some of the other highlights will include decorating a character shaped cake, shape clowns with icing, create a floral spray with roses, buds and drop flowers, writing in icing and more.

Intermediate Cake Decorating is a 5-session course, which requires the student to have the basic cake decorating. This course builds on the skills learned in the basic class. Some of the highlights of this course includes: basket weave technique, combining a variety of piping strokes to create new lavish borders and scrolls; gel transfers and edible wafer butterflies; elegant brush embroidery on a rolled fondant covered cake and many more.

Advanced Cake Decorating is 5 sessions and it is a requirement for the student to have taken both the basic and intermediate cake decorating. This course builds the decorating skills you learned in the first two cake decorating courses. This course will also highlight string work, garlands and new borders. The introduction to the royal icing – lattice and lace net piping; 3-D centerpiece; rolled fondant covered package cake with cutout inlay are also included. Along with 3-D butter cream/cake sculpture and fun with run sugar.

Tiered Wedding & Party Cakes is a one all-day session and each student must have decorating experience to take this class. This is a hands-on class, which focuses on how to support, stack, and tier and transport cakes. The pricing of cakes will be discussed for those who are want to own a business. Each student will have their choice of decorating a wedding or a party cake with a design of their choice. The cake must be 3 cake tiers – 6", 9" & 12".

Royal Icing Flowers – Lily & Flat Nail is a 3-session weekday class or an all-day Saturday class. Basic class or prior decorating experience is a necessity. The class is cover how to reduce last minute decorating stress and increase arranging option by making flowers ahead of time. Some of the flowers featured are: violet, pansy, daffodil, daisy, dogwood, primrose, lily, petunia, Vanda orchid and more.

Rose Review is a 1-session class. Students must have attended a Basic decorating class or have prior decorating experience. You will have the opportunity to improve on your piping skill and technique. You will be practicing your piping of roses and buds in this hands-on class.

Chocolate Fondant Grooms Cake is a one all-day Saturday session. It is a full day filled with new ideas and new techniques to embellish on the chocolate groom's cakes. This class can help set free your creativity and build on your decorating skills. Many of the same techniques can be used on other types of cakes. Working with fondant and butter cream methods will be covered.

Cup Cakes is a 1-session which will help you master the art of icing your cupcakes in a smooth and uniform manner.

Butter Cream Flowers is a 3-session course. Students must have attended a Basic Cake Decorating class before taking this class. In this class you will learn to pipe flowers directly onto the cake. The flowers being highlighted in this class are the lily, wisteria, Cattleya orchid, sweet pea and many more. You can also take this class as an all-day Saturday class.

All Day Basic Cake Decorating consists of orientation on Friday night and all-day Saturday session. This is more of a refresher course for those who may have taken a class many years before. This is a condensed class, which moves along rapidly for those who cannot take the 5-week series. Because of the reduced amount of time, not all of the regular Basic curriculum will be covered. Orientation will cover information on basic decorating tools; how to make the decorating icing; how to level, tort, fill and frost the cake. You will have hands on decorating covering the top and bottom borders; introduction to basic figure piping; piped roses & leaves; and more.

All Day Intermediate Cake Decorating is an all-day Saturday session, and all students must have Basic or All Day Basic Cake Decorating to attend. This is a condensed class, which moves at a rapid pace and is intended for those who cannot take the 5-week series. Because of the reduced amount of time, not all of the regular intermediate curriculum will be covered. Highlights will include new borders, piping gel transfers, and edible wafer butterflies and more.

All Day Chocolate Butter Cream Grooms Cake is a full day packed with new ideas and techniques for decorating the groom's cake using butter cream. The techniques can also be used on other occasion cakes.

Air Brush is a 4-session class and you must have basic and intermediate cake decorating instruction to attend. In this class you will learn to maximize your airbrush and create special effects on cakes and cookies. Highlights of the class are the operation and the care of the airbrush system; practice and control when using the system; applying food safe colors to enhance designs; how to cut and use custom stencils; and complete a portrait and more.

3D Figure Piping is an all-day Saturday session and you must have basic and intermediate cake decorating to attend. You will learn how to use butter cream to create 3D animals, cone dolls, and bubblehead people. You will be able to replace the plastic figures by adding this technique to your repertoire.

Gum paste Flowers is a 3-session course. This course will highlight how to make and handle gum paste. This class will include making the white Christmas rose, Poinsettia with buds, leaves and fillers.

Gum paste – Novelty Techniques is a 3-session course, which will expand your knowledge of sugar art by learning and building on the basics of gum paste. Highlights of this class will be techniques, which include molding, simple 3D construction, plaques, logs, butterflies, application of color and textures, bows and more.

Fondant Draping is a 3-session course and you must have completed basic cake decorating before you can attend this class. You will learn to cover a 2-tiered cake with rolled fondant. The cakes will be stacked and overly decorated with fondant ribbon roses and small 5 petal flowers, fondant draping and topped with a striking 3D pom-pom fondant bow. Other procedures highlighted will be embossing and simple fondant borders.

Fondant Frills is a 3-session course where you must have completed Fondant Draping first. You will create elegant fondant embellishments, which can be used on rolled fondant and butter cream cakes. You will also create swags, frills, edible beads, tassels and roping. Learn how to use crimpers and the clay gun. A lovely rolled fondant rose, bud and leaves will be a special highlight.

Advanced Fondant is a 3-session course where you must have completed Fondant Draping and Fondant Frills. You will have the opportunity to create fun figures, which can be the focal point of your cake. Learn basic shapes to create a duck, a bride and groom teddy bear and more. You will be dressing the figures to match a special occasion, which adds to the possibilities and fun. You will learn the uses of Patchwork cutters, Tappets, to create fondant & Gum paste decorations for your cakes and cookies.

Chocolate Fondant Groom's Cake is a one all-day Saturday session, which is a day filled with thrilling ideas and new techniques to decorate the chocolate groom's cakes. This class can help you unleash your creativity and it will help you build on your decorating skills. Working with fondant and butter cream techniques will be used during this session. The completion of a Basic and Intermediate Cake Decorating is a requirement.

Fondant Novelty Cakes and More is 3-session course and the completion of Fondant Draping, Frills and Figures is a requirement. This class will explore ways to use rolled fondant for novelty cakes. Some of the featured highlights will include the making of a tuxedo cake, basic base relief figure, butterflies, small fondant box and much more.

Gingerbread Houses is a 2 or 3-session class depending on the season of the class. Previous decorating experience is a requirement for this class. Gingerbread houses are a classic, which is love by children and adults alike during Easter, Halloween, and the Christmas holidays. During this class you will have the opportunity to create and decorate on of these special centerpieces for your family.

Panorama Eggs is a one all-day Saturday session with a Friday night orientation. The class will feature the glitter and the sparkle of molded sugar. Hollow sugar-shell eggs with royal icing scenes will be created; plus tips and hints on using molded sugar during the remainder of the year. This will expand the possibilities as well as enhance your sugar skill.

Air Brush is a 4-session course. The completion of a Basic and Intermediate Cake Decorating course is a requirement. You will learn to maximize your airbrush to create special effects on your cakes and cookies. Highlights of the class will be the operation and care of the airbrush system. You will practice control and the method of applying food safe colors to enhance and decorate. You will also learn how to cut and use custom stencils, complete a portrait and more.

Royal Icing Flowers is a course offered as a 3-session weekday class or an all-day Saturday session. The completion of a Basic Cake

Decorating or prior decorating experience is a must. You will learn to reduce last minute stress and increase arranging options by piping lovely flowers ahead of time. Some flowers featured will be violets, pansy, daffodil, daisy, dogwood, primrose, lily, petunia, orchid and more.

Gourmet and Restaurant Desserts is a 3-session class. You will learn to make those great desserts you may have tried in your favorite restaurant. The desserts will include Crème brulee, fruit and frangipane flan; baked Alaska, European tortes and gateaux are just a few. You will receive recipes, demonstrations and hands-on instructions.

Cookie Decorating Demonstration is a 1-session class. It is a wonderful bonus to add to your decorating skills. You will learn how to select a 3D design; properly roll out, cut, and bake the cookie dough. Decorating techniques will include glazes, sugars, colored cookie dough and piping with butter cream and royal icings. At the end of the day you will have a beautiful, edible centerpiece or gift.

Hands-On Cookie Decorating is a 1-session course. It is preferred you have attended the Cookie Demonstration first, but prior decorating experience is helpful. This hands-on cookies class is full of decorating methods and ideas such as glazing, sprinkles, royal icing, run sugar, baked on colored cookie dough and more.

Chocolate Candy Confections is a 1-session class, which demonstrates uses the convenience of summer coating to create delicious and attractive candy. You will learn to melt, pour, mold and paint with colored coating. Goodies such as peanut butter cups, chocolate covered cherries, nut clusters, truffles, liquor centers and more will be highlighted during the demonstration.

Chocolate Artistry is a one all-day Saturday session with a Friday night orientation, which requires you to have completed a basic and intermediate cake decorating, and the candy demonstration is a plus. This is not a candy making class, but an opportunity to learn and create decorative chocolate bows and curls. You will also make tuxedo strawberries; filigree butterflies and 3D scroll centerpieces; chocolate lace and many more other ideas.

For more information see cakecarousel.com

Chapter 10

Cake Art Cake Decorating and Candy Making Classes

These classes use a large portion of Wilton school's teaching in their curriculum. However, their classes and teaches may differ slightly.

Cake Art I – Wilton Method Basic Cake Decorating Course is a four 2-hour session. For the beginners, you will learn the fundamentals of decorating tools, icings, stars, writing, figure piping roses, shell borders, floral spray, leaves, cake preparation, and basic icing methods. You will learn some practical ideas from instructor who will be sharing their experiences with you. Practicing at home between lessons is important to obtaining a solid base in basic Cake Decorating. The Wilton Certificate of Completion will be awarded to those students who attend the session faithfully.

Cake Art 2 – Wilton Method Advanced Cake Decorating Course is a four 2-hour session where you will review the basics, and then you will concentrate on flowers such as Rosebud, Lily of the Valley, Chrysanthemum, Violet, Apple Blossom, Victorian Rose, Daisy, Daffodil, Pansy, Primrose, color flow work along with basket weaving, rope borders and ferns. Your will bring an iced cake ready to be decorated with the designs you have just learned. The Wilton certificate of Completion will be awarded to those students who attended every session.

Cake Art 3 – Wilton Fondant and tiered Cake Decorating Course. This is a four 2-hour session, and it is required for you to have completed Course 1 and 2 to take this course. In this course you will review the basics, and cover extensively the borders, lace and embroidery; string work, garland, e-motion, ruffle, Tiered Cake assembly. Fondant coloring, storing, covering cake, curved hearts piped, Lily, Poinsettia, Petunia, and working with a cake divider set will also be covered. You will complete a fondant-covered cake during the class. The Wilton Certificate of Completion will be awarded to those students who are faithful in their attendance.

Cake Art's Tiered Wedding Cake Decorating and Assembly Course is a four 2-hour session. Student must have completed Courses 1 and 2 in order to take this course. In this course concentration on decorating and assembling a Tiered Cake for all occasions. Review of the basics along with a review of the embellished borders, side borders, lacework, lattice work, filigree, lace points, piping on net, color flow, tiered cake designing, measuring and dividing cake. A Tiered Cake using Styrofoam cake dummies will be completed during the class. Practice at home will improve your skills. A Wilton certificate of Completion will be given to all students attending every session.

Wilton Basic Gum Paste is a class about the use of one of the most decorative skills, which can now be mastered by any cake decorator. Cutters and molds allow students to accomplish the professional effect in a fairly short amount of time. The classes will teach the basics of making the paste, the use of the tools, and cutting and molding some of the popular flowers. The fourth lesson will cover arranging the flowers into bouquets and corsages.

Gum Paste II - For this class, students must have completed the basic knowledge of gum paste course. You will do even more creative work with gum paste using the 75-piece JEM

Cutter set. You will create popular and seasonal flowers.

Wilton Orchid & Quick Rose Bouquets – For this class you must have completed a class on the basic knowledge of gum paste. The new Wilton Orchid and Quick Rose Cutter sets will be used in this class. Students will finish a rose and an orchid arrangement in this class.

Wilton Basic Rolled Fondant is a class where you will learn the graceful art of covering a cake with rolled fondant, giving it a very smooth iced surface. You will also learn to hand mold roses, how to complement the cake with crimping, frills and bead or rope borders.

Wilton "Victorian Fantasy" Fondant Class – For this class the student must have completed the basic knowledge of rolled fondant class. You will be decorating your fondant covered cake with the new Romantic Accents and Classic Accents Mold sets, along with many other techniques.

Butter Cream Rose Workshop – For this class the student must have a basic knowledge of cake decorating. In this class there will be a review for those that need it. In this class you will learn different methods of making icing roses by working with different petal tips. Students will learn to make miniature to giant roses.

Marzipan is a class using marzipan as a medium to teach the molding of fruits, vegetables, flowers and animals.

Basic Candy Making is a class where the instructor will show you how to mold chocolate, make simple chocolate covered candies, crunches and chocolate covered cherries. You will also learn how to make peanut butter cups, peppermint patties, and more.

Fruit and Vegetable Garnish is a class where you will make your food look as good as it tastes. Learn the tips to successful garnishing. Choosing the right ingredients and tools. You want the garnish to compliment the dish and how to store until you are ready to use them.

Wilton Cookie Bouquet where you will make an edible cookie blossom centerpiece. This class will cover baking, decorating, and arrangement of cookies to make bouquets for almost any occasion.

Wilton Sugar Molding (Panoramic)

In this class you will learn to mold and decorate hollow sugar ornaments for centerpieces, party favors, and cake decorations. Your lessons will correspond with the season.

Gingerbread House

With this class you will be able to surprise your family and ficnds with a gingerbread house. This gingerbread you will have made and decorated yourself. This class is about baking, constructing and decorating this beautiful, edible centerpiece.

Chapter 11

Golda's Kitchen

Golda's Kitchen is located in Canada and offers Decorating Courses. She believes whether you are a novice or an expert you can always learn something in a cooking class. Golda's Kitchen offers Cake Decorating classes.

Decorating Classes

Whether you are baking a cake from scratch or using a mix, there is a way to turn every cake and dessert into something special by using some simple decorating techniques.

Cake Decorating I

Discover Cake Decorating

This is an introductory course, which will cover everything from the basics of icing a cake to creating the lovely borders, stars and shells. We will also cover writing, figure piping, and making icing roses and floral sprays. This is the perfect way to learn to decorate cakes for a birthday or a bridal or baby shower. You make and decorate two cakes and a wide range of cupcakes during the course of this class. You will receive hands-on guidance in torting, smoothly icing, and combing your cakes, and extra instruction on figure piping a variety of cute characters.

Cake Decorating II

Flowers and Borders

This course will build on the basics you learned in Cake Decorating I and introduce you to impressive techniques to make your cakes unforgettable You will be able to master new borders, which feature rosettes, reverse shells, and rope designs. This will give your cakes dimension with the addition of color flow decoration. You will be able to make wonderful flowers, including rosebuds, daisies, daffodils, mum, pansies, sunflowers, zinnias, and ferns, and you will be able to use them to create your grand finale. Your grand finale will be a flower basket cake using basket weave technique.

Cake Decorating III

Fondant and Tiered Cakes

In this course you will learn detailed accents such as embroidery and lace, string work, garland, ruffle borders, and overpiping. You will discover the beauty of covering cakes with rolled fondant, which gives the cake a perfectly smooth surface and shaping fun figures and beautiful flowers. You will add more icing flowers to your repertoire. Some of these are poinsettias, Easter lilies, and petunias. You will complete the course by assembling and decorating a towering tiered cake with all the decorations you have learned so far.

Fondant and Gum Paste

With rolled fondant and gum paste, there is absolutely no limit to the decorations you can make for your cakes. These thick like icing are easy to cut and shape to create wonderful flowers and beautifully- textured drapes and borders. You will learn how to properly handle, cut, and tint fondant and gum paste. You will also learn to cover a cake and board with fondant and add effects such as ribbon garland, rope borders, punched strips, inlays, and appliqués. You will also create a variety of gum paste flowers, including daisies, carnations, and leaves.

Elegant Fondant: Tiered Cakes

You will learn the necessary skills to assemble and decorate a fondant-covered tiered cake, such as wedding cakes.

Gum Paste Flowers I

Learn to make lifelike flowers out of gum paste. You will be able to create a bouquet of popular flowers and foliage to enhance any cake, including roses, daisies, calla lilies, orchids, sweet peas, carnations, daffodils, small blossoms and leaves.

Gum Paste Flowers II

Learn to make even more lifelike flowers out of gum paste.

Fun with Cookies I

You will learn the techniques to decorating cookies, suitable for gift giving and holiday decorations. Egg wash, glaze, cookie icing, butter cream icing, and run sugar icing and color flow will be used to cover the cookies. You will be decorating with colored sugars, sprinkles, glitter, dragees, and luster dusts.

Fun with Cookies II

You will continue to cover the techniques suitable for decorating cookies, for gift giving and holiday decorations. Candy coating, fondant, and other advanced techniques will be used to decorate these cookies.

Fun with Cupcakes

You will learn techniques used in decorating cupcakes. These cupcakes will be suitable for parties, weddings, or holiday treats. Butter cream icing and fondant will be used to cover and decorate these cupcakes. You will use the piping skills you learned in previous classes.

Chapter 12

Open Directory

The Pastry Wiz is one of the many listing you will find in the open directory, but it also has its own web site. The Pastry Wiz has a lot of information about wedding cakes, including the history, but if you look more, you will find a web page, which has many other listing ranging from Halloween to the directions of making a swan out of blown sugar and a flower from pulled sugar.

The Sugar Artistry

This section of the Pastry Wiz will show you, in step-by-step instructions, how to blow sugar in order for you to create a beautiful swan. First they will show you the ingredients and supplies you will need and then they show you all the steps for the cooking, handling, pulling and blowing of the sugar, so you can create your own masterpiece.

Cake Decorating

For Christmas, they will show you how to make a stand-up Santa Claus and Rudolph cake. As with everything, they will tell you the ingredients and supplies needed to make the cake and decorate it.

You can also make with their instruction a Christening Cradle – a Baby Crib Decoration or maybe you would rather make a kissing frog on a Valentine's Cake, or even a Thanksgiving Turkey Cake.

For Halloween you can get step-by-step instructions on how to make a Dracula or and bat cake, or you can use one of their many other Halloween ideas. You download the instructions. They will tell you the supplies you need so you can have them all together, and viola you are in business.

They have instructions on how to decorate using a paper cone, and how to decorate petit fours. They also have instructions on crystallizing or sugar coating flowers and how to writing messages on your cake. They will show you how to make marzipan elephants for the kids.

They will even help you pick out a wedding cake or tell you how you can make one. There is no end to the number of ideas this web site has in making edible decorations.

If you want to make a Victorian Decorated Wedding Cake they have the instructions for that one too!

They even have recipes for pies. They will instruct you step-by-step on how to make and assemble an apple pie.

They have recipes for European cookies. They will help you make gifts for Christmas with jars and cookies, and cakes. They will help you step-by-step assemble and decorate a gingerbread house.

These lessons all seem to be for the person who has already received basic training in cake decorating, but they can help you hone your skills and sharpen your expertise.

Bake Decorate Celebrate is another one of the links you can open when visiting the open directory. It has projects, techniques, recipes, and a cake-decorating forum.

Baking 911: Cake Decorating is a link, which offers step-by-step cake decorating including leveling, filling, icing, glazes and recipes. They have basic instructions and other instructions as well.

Cake Decorating Corner another link, which has cake decorating photos with detailed instructions. It has also decorating techniques, homemade cake recipes, and icing recipes.

The Cake Journal has techniques, recipes, and general information about cake decorating and sugar craft. It is presented in weblog format.

Cake Central.com has cake decorating ideas, photo galleries, tutorials, and recipes. This is a great web site for the cake enthusiasts.

Good Housekeeping Cake Tips is a great guide for the cake decorating beginners.

Kimberly Chapman's Cake Decorating has recipes and how-to's for sugar craft and cake decorating. This web site includes sources for necessary ingredients.

Sugar Buzz is a cake decorating community with users sharing recipes, ideas, and pictures.

Tanzicakes is a web hosted by a Wilton instructor who is still teaching. There are cakes decorating ideas and the instructions on how-to accomplish them. It also includes decorated cake photos.

Wilton Cupcake Stand, this web site will have everything you ever wanted to know about the Wilton Cupcake stand. This web site is for blogs and forums to talk about the cupcake stand.

Wilton Recipes and Projects is a web site with decorating tips, recipes, and basic decorating instructions.

Chapter 13

Fabulous Foods and Cakes N Things

This web site is all about cooking and teaching how to cook. Even though they have several cooking locations on their web site, they do have one, which deals with cake decorating.

How to Make Multi-Colored Borders

If you want to know how to make two and three color borders then you need to check out the instructions on this web site.

How to Decorate Cookies

In this page of the web site, you will learn how to line and then fill in the area of the cookie you want iced. Royal icing is used for these sugar cookies and they have a great sugar cookie recipe you can print from your computer.

Decorated Cakes

Making cakes look good isn't hard if you know a few tricks of the trade, and you have the right tools. One of the things you will want to know is how to bake a flat cake. You know every time you bake a cake the cake will come out with a domed top, which you will have to cut to level the cake before you can decorate it.

The first thing you do after you have filled your cake pans is to tap them on the counter a few times. This will help eliminate any air bubbles in the batter. But that is not all. You will need to take a dishtowel (you might want to use an old one) and wet it. Fold the towel and wrap it around the outside of your cake pan and fasten with a safety pin. The moist heat from the towel helps the cake bake, but it will also rise more evenly. You might want to save the towel. It can be used again. If you prefer, you can purchase an insulated cake pan from the cake-decorating store, but the towel method will work as well.

Filling a pastry bag, if you have ever done it, is a messy job. Here is a way to cut down on the mess. Place your pastry bag inside a tall kitchen glass and fold the ends over the top of the glass. Then just spoon the icing into the bag.

The quickest and easiest way to ice the sides of a cake, is to fill a large pastry bag with a giant size tip. It will make icing the sides of the cake much easier.

To ice you cake so as to have a smooth canvas to start your decorations on, just follow along here. Place your cake on a cake board or plate. If you need to, you can use the icing as a glue to glue the cake to the board or plate, in order to keep it from sliding.

Next using an offset spatula, spread a layer of icing over the top of the bottom layer, and then set the second layer on top.

Spread icing over the top of the newly added layer. Since you do not want any crumbs in the icing, always push your spatula outwards. Pulling back will allow you to pick up crumbs. Also start with a large blob of icing in the middle of the cake and spread outward. Don't worry about adding too much icing, you can use the spatula to scrap some off later. By starting off with a large amount of frosting also makes it easier to smooth the icing finish. Then use a large pastry bag with the giant size tip to ice the sides of the cake. Smooth out the icing with your spatula.

The ebay Basic Cake Decorating web site is a web site, which will teach you all the basics of cake decorating with step-by-step instructions. This web site will go over all the tools you will need for your cake decorating.

Show you a picture and explain what the tool is used for. All of the tools and equipment they will show you can be found in an craft and hobby store, such as Michael's or in a cake decorating store. There are also several locations on the web where cake-decorating supplies are sold.

They will give you the recipes you will need to use for your practice in using these tools, and give you practice sessions you can follow. They will walk you through each step of the tips, pastry bag and all the other tools you will need in your cake decorating kit.

They also have downloadable instructions on how to use the Wilton novelty and character pans. This web site is one of the best web site for beginners in cake decorating. If you have never taken a cake decorating class, this is a great on for those just starting out. If you do not need a human's guidance in learn cake decorating, this will work for you.

Cake decorating can be a great hobby. If you would like to start your own business, this is a great business to get into. There are many people who love beautifully decorated cakes, but do not have the knowledge or maybe the time to do it for themselves. You can even go so far as to earn a degree and work in 5-star hotel and restaurants or even own your own bakery and enjoy a good living from your skills.

Whatever you decide to do, the door is open wide and all you have to do is to walk through it. Good Luck!

Cake Decorating for Beginners

CPSIA information can be obtained
at www.ICGtesting.com
Printed in the USA
LVHW081142221122
733792LV00021B/262